1970

This book may be k

AMERICAN EDUCATION

Its Men

Ideas

and

Institutions

Advisory Editor

Lawrence A. Cremin
Frederick A. P. Barnard Professor of Education
Teachers College, Columbia University

The Educational Situation

John Dewey

ARNO PRESS & THE NEW YORK TIMES
*New York * 1969*

Reprint edition 1969 by Arno Press, Inc.

*

Library of Congress Catalog Card No. 71-89173

*

Reprinted from a copy in Teachers College Library

*

Manufactured in the United States of America

Editorial Note

AMERICAN EDUCATION: *Its Men, Institutions and Ideas* presents selected works of thought and scholarship that have long been out of print or otherwise unavailable. Inevitably, such works will include particular ideas and doctrines that have been outmoded or superseded by more recent research. Nevertheless, all retain their place in the literature, having influenced educational thought and practice in their own time and having provided the basis for subsequent scholarship.

Lawrence A. Cremin
Teachers College

The Educational Situation

The Educational Situation

BY

JOHN DEWEY

PROFESSOR AND HEAD OF THE DEPARTMENT OF PHILOSOPHY AND
DIRECTOR OF THE SCHOOL OF EDUCATION IN
THE UNIVERSITY OF CHICAGO

CONTRIBUTIONS TO EDUCATION
NUMBER III

SECOND EDITION

CHICAGO
THE UNIVERSITY OF CHICAGO PRESS
1904

PREFATORY WORD.

In the following paper I have attempted to set forth the educational situation as it manifests itself in the three typical parts of our educational system. In so doing, I have revised papers originally prepared for three different bodies, namely, the Superintendent's section of the National Educational. Association; the Conference of Secondary Schools affiliated with the University of Chicago; and the Harvard Teachers Association. If the following paper in the reading leaves with the reader the impression of a miscellaneous collection, not of an organic unity, it will hardly be worth while for me here to iterate that it is an attempt to apply a single social philosophy, a single educational philosophy, to a single problem manifested in forms that are only outwardly diverse. I may, however, be allowed to say that in each case I have tried to interpret the particular member of the school organism dealt with in its twofold relation: to the past which has determined its conditions and forms ; and to the present which determines its aims and results — its ideals and its success or failure in realizing them. The school more than any one other social institution stands between the past and the future; it is the living present as reflection of the past and as prophecy of the future. To this is due the intensity of intellectual and moral interest attaching to all that concerns the school—if only our eyes are open to see.

JOHN DEWEY.

THE UNIVERSITY OF CHICAGO.
December 12, 1901.

THE EDUCATIONAL SITUATION.

I. AS CONCERNS THE ELEMENTARY SCHOOL.

HORACE MANN and the disciples of Pestalozzi did their peculiar missionary work so completely as intellectually to crowd the conservative to the wall. For half a century after their time the ethical emotion, the bulk of exhortation, the current formulæ and catchwords, the distinctive principles of theory have been found on the side of progress, of what is known as reform. The supremacy of self-activity, the symmetrical development of all the powers, the priority of character to information, the necessity of putting the real before the symbol, the concrete before the abstract, the necessity of following the order of nature and not the order of human convention — all these ideas, at the outset so revolutionary, have filtered into the pedagogic consciousness and become the commonplace of pedagogic writing and of the gatherings where teachers meet for inspiration and admonition.

It is, however, sufficiently obvious that, while the reformer took possession of the field of

9

theory and enthusiasm and preaching, the
conservative, so far as concerns the course
of study was holding his own pretty obsti-
nately in the region of practice. He could
afford to neglect all these sayings; nay, he
could afford to take a part in a glib reiter-
ation of the shibboleths, because, as a
matter of fact, his own work remained so
largely untouched. He retained actual control of school conditions; it was he who
brought about the final and actual contact
between the theories and the child. And by
the time ideals and theories had been trans-
lated over into their working equivalents in
the curriculum, the difference between them
and what he as a conservative really wished
and practiced became often the simple difference of tweedle dum from tweedle dee. So
the "great big battle" was fought with mutual
satisfaction, each side having an almost complete victory in its own field. Where the reformer made his headway was not in the
region of studies, but rather in that of methods
and of atmosphere of school-work.

In the last twenty or twenty-five years, however, more serious attempts have been made
to carry the theory into effective execution
in subject-matter as well as in method. The
unconscious insincerity in continually turning

the theory over and over in terms of itself, the unconscious self-deceit in using it simply to cast an idealized and emotional halo over a mechanical school routine with which it was fundamentally at odds, became somewhat painfully apparent; consequently the effort to change the concrete school materials and school subject-matter so as to give the professed ends and aims a *pou sto* within the school walls and in relation to the children.

Drawing, music, nature study with the field excursion and the school garden, manual training, the continuation of the constructive exercises of the kindergarten, the story and the tale, the biography, the dramatic episode, and anniversary of heroic history found their way into the schoolrooms. We, they proclaim, are the working counterparts of the commands to follow nature; to secure the complete development of the child; to present the real before the symbolic, etc. Interest was transferred from the region of pedagogic principles and ideals, as such, to the child as affected by these principles and ideas. The formulæ of pedagogics were reduced in importance, and the present experience of the child was magnified. The gospel of the emancipation of the child succeeded the gospel of the emancipation of the educational theorist. This gospel was

published abroad, and verily its day seemed at
hand. It was apparently only a question of
pushing a few more old fogies out of the way,
and waiting for others to pass out of existence in the natural course of events, and the
long-wished-for educational reformation would
be accomplished.

Needless to say, the affair was not quite so
simple. The conservative was still there. He
was there not only as a teacher in the schoolroom, but he was there in the board of education; he was there because he was still in the
heart and mind of the parent; because he still
possessed and controlled the intellectual and
moral standards and expectations of the community. We began to learn that an educational reform is but one phase of a general
social modification.

Moreover, certain evils began to show
themselves. Studies were multiplied almost
indefinitely, often overtaxing the physical and
mental strength of both teacher and child,
leading to a congestion of the curriculum, to a
distraction and dissipation of aim and effort on
the part of instructor and pupil. Too often
an excess of emotional excitement and strain
abruptly replaced the former apathy and dull
routine of the school. There were complaints
in every community of loss of efficiency in the

older studies, and of a letting down of the seri-
ousness of mental training. It is not necessary to consider how well founded these
objections have been. The fact that they are
so commonly made, the fact that these newer
studies are often regarded simply as fads and
frills, is sufficient evidence of the main point,
viz., of the external and mechanical position
occupied by these studies in the curriculum.
Numbers of cities throughout the country point
the moral. When the winds blew and the rains
fell — in the shape of a financial stringency in
the community and the business conduct of
the school — the new educational edifice too
often fell. It may not have been built entirely
upon the sand, but at all events it was not
founded upon a rock. The taxpayer spoke,
and somehow the studies which represented the
symmetrical development of the child and the
necessity of giving him the concrete before
the abstract went into eclipse.

   It is, of course, agreeable for those who
believe in progress, in reform, in new ideals, to
attribute these reactions to a hard and stiff-
necked generation who willfully refuse to
recognize the highest goods when they see
them. It is agreeable to regard such as
barbarians who are interested simply in turning back the wheels of progress. The simple

fact, however, is that education is the one
thing in which the American people believe
without reserve, and to which they are without
reserve committed. Indeed, I sometimes think
that the necessity of education is the only
settled article in the shifting and confused
social and moral creed of America. If, then,
the American public fails, in critical cases, to
stand by the educational newcomers, it is because these latter have not yet become organic
parts of the educational whole — otherwise
they could not be cut out. They are not really
in the unity of educational movement — otherwise they could not be arrested. They are
still insertions and additions.

Consider the wave by which a new study is
introduced into the curriculum. Someone feels
that the school system of his (or quite frequently nowadays her) town is falling behind
the times. There are rumors of great progress in education making elsewhere. Something new and important has been introduced;
education is being revolutionized by it; the
school superintendent, or members of the board
of education, become somewhat uneasy; the
matter is taken up by individuals and clubs;
pressure is brought to bear on the managers of
the school system; letters are written to the
newspapers; the editor himself is appealed to

to use his great power to advance the cause of progress; editorials appear; finally the school board ordains that on and after a certain date the particular new branch—be it nature study, industrial drawing, cooking, manual training, or whatever—shall be taught in the public schools. The victory is won, and everybody —unless it be some already overburdened and distracted teacher—congratulates everybody else that such advanced steps are taking.

The next year, or possibly the next month, there comes an outcry that children do not write or spell or figure as well as they used to; that they cannot do the necessary work in the upper grades, or in the high school, because of lack of ready command of the necessary tools of study. We are told that they are not prepared for business, because their spelling is so poor, their work in addition and multiplication so slow and inaccurate, their handwriting so fearfully and wonderfully made. Some zealous soul on the school board takes up *this* matter; the newspapers are again heard from; investigations are set on foot; and the edict goes forth that there must be more drill in the fundamentals of writing, spelling, and number.

Moreover, in the last year or two there are many signs that the older and traditional studies do not propose to be ignored. For a long time, as already intimated, the conservative was, upon the whole, quite content to surrender the intellectual and emotional territory, the sphere of theory and of warmly toned ideals, to the reformer. He was content because he, after all, remained in possession of the field of action. But now there are symptoms of another attitude; the conservative is, so to speak, coming to intellectual and moral consciousness himself. He is asserting that in his conservatism he stands for more than the mere customs and traditions of an outworn past. He asserts that he stands for honesty of work, for stability, for thoroughness, for singleness of aim and concentration of agencies, for a reasonable simplicity. He is actively probing the innovator. He is asking questions regarding the guarantees of personal and intellectual discipline, of power of control, of ability to work. He is asking whether there is not danger of both teacher and child getting lost amid the portentous multiplication of studies. He is asking about the leisure requisite to intellectual and mental digestion, and subsequent growth. He is asking whether there is not danger to integrity of character in arousing so many interests and impulses that no one of them is carried through to an effective result. These are not matters of mere school procedure or formal arrangement of studies, but matters fundamental to intellectual and moral achievement. Moreover, some recent magazine articles seem to indicate that some few, at least, of the reformers are themselves beginning to draw back; they are apparently wondering if this new-created child of theirs be not a Frankenstein, which is to turn and rend its creator. They seem to be saying: "Possibly we are in danger of going too fast and too far; what and where are the limits of this thing we are entered upon?"

My sketch, however inadequate, is yet, I hope, true to the logic, if not to the details, of history. What emerges from this running account ? What does it all mean ? Does it not signify that we have a situation in process of forming rather than a definitive situation? The history reflects both our lack of intellectual organization and also the increasing recognition of the factors which must enter into any such organization. From this point of view, the renewed self-assertion, from the standpoint of theory, of the adherents of the traditional curriculum is a matter of congratulation. It shows that we are emerging from a period of practical struggle to that of intellectual interpretation and adjustment. As yet, however, we have no conscious educational standard by which to test and place each aspiring claimant. We have hundreds of reasons for and against this or that study, but no reason. Having no sense of the unity of experience, and of the definitive relation of each branch of study to that unity, we have no criterion by which to judge and decide. We yield to popular pressure and clamor; first on the side of the instinct for progress, and then on the side of the habit of inertia. As a result, every movement, whether for nature study or spelling, for picture study or arithmetic, for manual training or more legible handwriting, is treated as an isolated and independent thing. It is this separation, this lack of vital unity, which leads to the confusion and contention which are so marked features of the educational situation. Lacking a philosophy of unity, we have no basis upon which to make connections, and our whole treatment becomes piecemeal, empirical and at the mercy of external circumstances.

The problem of the course of study is thus, in effect, a part of the larger problem so pressing in all departments of the organization of life. Everywhere we have outgrown old methods and standards; everywhere we are crowded by new resources, new instrumentalities; we are bewildered by the multitude of new oppor-

tunities that present themselves. Our difficulties of today come, not from paucity or
poverty, but from the multiplication of means
clear beyond our present powers of use and
administration. We have got away from the
inherited and customary; we have not come
into complete possession and command of the
present. Unification, organization, harmony, is
the demand of every aspect of life—politics,
business, science. That education shares in
the confusion of transition, and in the demand
for reorganization, is a source of encouragement and not of despair. It proves how inte-
grally the school is bound up with the entire
movement of modern life.

The situation thus ceases to be a conflict between what is called the old education and the
new. There is no longer any old education.
save here and there in some belated geo-
graphic area. There is no new education in
definite and supreme existence. What we
have is certain vital tendencies. These tendencies ought to work together ; each stands
for a phase of reality and contributes a factor
of efficiency. But because of lack of organization, because of the lack of unified insight
upon which organization depends, these tendencies are diverse and tangential. Too often
we have their mechanical combination and

irrational compromise. More prophetic, because more vital, is the confusion which arises
from their conflict. We have been putting
new wine into old bottles, and that which was
prophesied has come to pass.

To recognize that the situation is not the
wholesale antagonism of so-called old education to the so-called new, but a question of
the co-operative adjustment of necessary factors in a common situation, is to surrender our
partisanship. It is to cease our recriminations
and our self-conceits, and search for a more
comprehensive end than is represented by
either factor apart from the other. It is impossible to anticipate the exact and final outcome of this search. Only time, and the light
that comes with time, can reveal the answer.
The first step, however, is to study the existing situation as students, not as partisans,
and, having located the vital factors in it, consider what it is that makes them at the present
juncture antagonistic competitors instead of
friendly co-operators.

The question is just this : Why do the newer
studies, drawing, music, nature study, manual
training ; and the older studies, the three R's,
practically conflict with, instead of reinforcing,
one another ? Why is it that the practical
problem is so often simply one of outward

annexation or mechanical compromise? Why
is it that the adjustment of the conflict is left
to the mere push and pull of contending factors, to the pressure of local circumstances
and of temporary reactions ?

An answer to this question is, I believe, the
indispensable preliminary to any future understanding. Put roughly, we have two groups
of studies ; one represents the symbols of the
intellectual life, which are the tools of civilization itself; the other group stands for the
direct and present expression of power on the
part of one undergoing education, and for the
present and direct enrichment of his life-ex-
perience. For reasons historically adequate,
the former group represents the traditional
education ; the latter, the efforts of the innovator. Intrinsically speaking, in the abstract,
there is no reason to assume any fundamental,
or even any minor, antagonism between these
two groups. Such an assumption would mean
that the requirements of civilization are fundamentally at war with the conditions of individual development ; that the agencies by
which society maintains itself are at radical
odds with the forms by which individual experience is deepened and expanded. Unless
we are ready to concede such a fundamental
contradiction in the make-up of life, we must

hold that the present contention is the result of conditions which are local and transitory.

I offer the following proposition as giving the key to the conflict :

The studies of the symbolic and formal sort represented the aims and material of education for a sufficiently long time to call into existence a machinery of administration and of instruction thoroughly adapted to themselves. This machinery constituted the actual working scheme of administration and instruction. These conditions persist long after the studies to which they are well adapted have lost their theoretical supremacy. The conflict, the confusion, the compromise, is not intrinsically between the older group of studies and the newer, but between the external conditions in which the former were realized and the aims and standards represented by the newer.

It is easy to fall into the habit of regarding the mechanics of school organization and administration as something comparatively external and indifferent to educational purposes and ideals. We think of the grouping of children in classes, the arrangement of grades, the machinery by which the course of study is made out and laid down, the method by which it is carried into effect, the system of selecting teachers and of assigning them to their work, of paying and promoting them, as, in a way, matters of mere practical convenience and expediency. We forget that it is precisely such things as these that really control the whole system, even on its distinctively educational side. No matter what is the accepted precept and theory, no matter what the legislation of the school board or the mandate of the school superintendent, the reality of education is found in the personal and face-to-face contact of teacher and child. The conditions that underlie and regulate this contact dominate the educational situation.

In this contact, and in it alone, can the reality of current education be got at. To get away from it is to be ignorant and to deceive ourselves. It is in this contact that the real course of study, whatever be laid down on paper, is actually found. Now, the conditions that determine this personal contact of child with child, and of children with teacher are, upon the whole, the survival of the period when the domination of the three R's was practically unquestioned. Their effectiveness lies in their adaptation to realizing the ends and aims of that form of education. They do not lend themselves to realizing the purposes of the newer studies. Consequently we do not get the full benefit either of the old or of the

new studies. They work at cross purposes.
The excellence which the conditions would
possess if they were directed solely at securing
progress in reading, writing, and arithmetic,
and allied topics, is lost because of the introduction of material irrelevant and distracting
from the standpoint of the conditions. The new
studies do not have an opportunity to show
what they can do, because they are hampered
by machinery constructed for turning out another kind of goods; they are not provided
with their own distinctive set of agencies.
Granted this contradiction, the only wonder is
that the chaos is not greater than it actually
is; the only wonder is that we are securing
such positive results as actually come about.

Let us study this contradiction somewhat
more intimately, taking up one by one some
of its constituent elements. On the side of
the machinery of school-work I mention first
the number of children in a room. This runs
in the graded schools of our country anywhere
from thirty-five to sixty. This can hardly be
said to be an ideal condition, even from the
standpoint of uniform progress in reading,
writing, and arithmetic, and the symbols of
geography and history; but it certainly is
indefinitely better adapted to securing these
results than that of the symmetrical and com-

plete development of all the powers, physical, mental, moral, æsthetic, of each individual child out of the entire fifty. From the standpoint of the latter aim, the discrepancy is so great that the situation is either ridiculous or tragic. Under such circumstances, how do we have the face to continue to speak at all of the complete development of the individual as the supreme end of educational effort? Excepting here and there with the genius who seems to rise above all conditions, the school environment and machinery almost compel the more mechanical features of school-work to lord it over the more vital aims.

We get the same result when we consider, not the number of children in a given grade, but the arrangement of grades. The distribution into separate years, each with its own distinctive and definite amount of ground to be covered, the assignment of one and only one teacher to a grade, the confinement of the same teacher to the same grade year by year, save as she is "promoted" to a higher grade, introduce an isolation which is fatal, I will not say to good work, but to the effective domination of the ideal of continuous development of character and personal powers. The unity and wholeness of the child's development can be realized only in a corresponding unity and continuity of school conditions. Anything that breaks the latter up into fractions, into isolated parts, must have the same influence upon the educative growth of the child.[1]

It may, however, be admitted that these conditions, while highly important as regards the aims of education, have little or nothing to do with the course of study—with the subject-matter of instruction. But a little reflection will show that the material of study is profoundly affected. The conditions which compel the children to be dealt with *en masse*, which compel them to be led in flocks, if not in hordes, make it necessary to give the stress of attention to those studies in which some sort of definite result can be most successfully attained, without much appeal to individual initiative, judgment, or inquiry. Almost of necessity, attention to the newer studies whose value is dependent upon personal appropriation, assimilation and expression is incidental and superficial. The results with the latter are naturally often so unsatisfactory that they are held responsible for the evil consequences; we fail to trace the matter back to the conditions which control the result reached. Upon the

[1] This thought is developed in the first number of this series: *Isolation in the School*, especially pp. 33–40 ; 92–98.

whole, it is testimony to the vitality of these studies that in such a situation the results are not worse than they actually are.

Unless the teacher has opportunity and occasion to study the educative process as a whole, not as divided into eight or twelve or sixteen parts, it is impossible to see how he can deal effectively with the problem of the complete development of the child. The restriction of outlook to one limited year of the child's growth will inevitably tend in one of two directions : either the teacher's work becomes mechanical, because practically limited to covering the work assigned for the year, irrespective of its nutritive value in the child's growth ; or else local and transitory phases of the child's development are seized upon — phases which too often go by the name of the interests of the child — and these are exaggerated out of all due bounds. Since the newer studies give most help in making this excessive and sensational appeal, these studies are held responsible for the evils that subsequently show themselves. As a matter of fact, the cause of the difficulty lies in the isolation and restriction of the work of the teacher which practically forbids his considering the significance of art, music, and nature study in the light of continuity and completeness of growth.

This unity and completeness must, however, be cared for somehow. Since not provided for on the basis of the teacher's knowledge of the whole process of which his own work is one organic member, it is taken care of through external provision of a consecutive course of study, external supervision, and the mechanics of examination and promotion. Connection must somehow be made between the various fractional parts — the successive grades. The supervisor, the principal, is the recourse. Acting, however, not through the medium of the consciousness of the class-room teacher, but through the medium of prescription of mode of action, the inevitable tendency is to arrest attention upon those parts of the subject-matter which lend themselves to external assignment and conjunction. Even music, drawing, and manual training are profoundly influenced by this fact. Their own vital aims and spirit are compromised, or even surrendered, to the necessities for laying out a course of study in such a manner that one year's work may fit externally into that of the next. Thus they part with much of their own distinctive and characteristic value, and become, to a considerable extent, simple additions to the number of routine studies carried by children and teacher. They serve no new purpose of their

own, but add to the burden of the old. It is
no wonder that, when the burden gets too
great, there is demand that they be lopped
off as excrescences upon the educational system.

The matter of promotion from grade to
grade has a precisely similar effect upon the
course of study. It is from the standpoint of
the child, just what the isolation and external
combination already alluded to are from the
side of the teacher. The things of the spirit
do not lend themselves easily to that kind of
external inspection which goes by the name
of examination. They do not lend themselves
easily to exact quantitative measurement.
Technical proficiency, acquisition of skill and
information, present much less difficulty. So
again emphasis is thrown upon those traditional subjects of the school curriculum which
permit most readily a mechanical treatment
—upon the three R's and upon the facts of
external classification in history and science,
matters of formal technique in music, drawing,
and manual training. Continuity, order, must
be somewhat maintained—if not the order
and method of the spirit, then at least that of
external conditions. Nothing is gained by
throwing everything into chaos. In this sense
the conservative is thoroughly right when he

insists upon the maintenance of the established traditions of the school as regards the tests of the pupil's ability and preparation for promotion. He fails, however, to recognize the other alternative : that the looseness and confusion, the vagueness in accomplishment and in test of accomplishment of which he complains, may be due, not to the new studies themselves, but to the unfit conditions under which they operate.

I have already alluded to the fact that at present the teacher is hardly enabled to get a glimpse of the educative process as a whole, and accordingly is reduced to adding together the various external bits into which that unity is broken. We get exactly the same result when we consider the way in which the course of study is determined. The fact that this is fixed by board of education, superintendent, or supervisor, by a power outside the teacher in the class room who alone can make that course of study a living reality, is a fact too obvious to be concealed. It is, however, comparatively easy to conceal from ourselves the tremendous import of this fact. As long as the teacher, who is after all the only real educator in the school system, has no definite and authoritative position in shaping the course of study, that is likely to remain an external thing to be externally applied to the child.[1]

A school board or a superintendent can lay out a course of study down to the point of stating exactly the number of pages of text-books to be covered in each year, each term and month of the year. It may prescribe the exact integers and fraction of integers with which the child shall make scholastic acquaint-ance during any period of 'his instruction; it may directly or indirectly define the exact shapes to be reproduced in drawing, or men-tion the exact recipes to be followed in cooking. Doubtless the experience of the individual teacher who makes the connections between these things and the life of the child will receive incidental attention in laying out these courses. But, so long as the teacher has no definite voice, the attention will be only incidental; and, as a further conse-quence, the average teacher will give only incidental study to the problems involved. If his work is the task of carrying out the instructions imposed upon him, then his time and thought must be absorbed in the matter of execution. There is no motive for interest, of a thoroughly vital and alert sort, in ques-tions of the intrinsic value of the subject-

[1] See, again, Number I of this series, pp. 31–32 and 106–109.

matter and its adaptation to the needs of child growth. He may be called upon by official requirements, or the pressure of circumstance, to be a student of pedagogical books and journals; but conditions relieve him of the necessity of being a student of the most fundamental educational problems in their most urgent reality.

The teacher needs to study the mechanics of successfully carrying into effect the prescribed matter of instruction; he does not have to study that matter itself, or its educative bearing. Needless to say, the effect of this upon the actual course of study is to emphasize the thought and time given to those subjects and phases of subjects where there is most promise of success in doing the exact things prescribed. The three R's are again magnified, while the technical and routine aspects of the newer studies tend to crowd out those elements that give them their deeper significance in intellectual and moral life. Since, however, the school must have relief from monotony, must have "interest," must have diversification and recreation, these studies become too easily tools for introducing the excitement and amusement supposed to be necessary. The judicious observer who sees below the surface, but not to the foundation, again discounts these studies. Meanwhile the actual efficiency of the three R's is hampered and lessened by the superaddition of the new ways of employing time, whether they be routine or exciting in character.

It may easily be said that the class-room teacher at present is not sufficiently educated to be intrusted with any part in shaping a course of study. I waive the fundamental question—the question of democracy—whether the needed education can be secured without giving more responsibility even to the comparatively uneducated. The objection suggests another fundamental condition in our present school procedure—the question of the status of the teacher as regards selection and appointment.

The real course of study must come to the child from the teacher. What gets to the child is dependent upon what is in the mind and consciousness of the teacher, and upon the way it is in his mind. It is through the teacher that the value even of what is contained in the text-book is brought home to the child; just in the degree in which the teacher's understanding of the material of the lessons is vital, adequate, and comprehensive, will that material come to the child in the same form; in the degree in which the teacher's understanding is mechanical, superficial and restricted, the child's appreciation will be correspondingly limited and perverted. If this be true, it is obviously futile to plan large expansions of the studies of the curriculum apart from the education of the teacher. I am far from denying the capacity on the part of truth above and beyond the comprehension of the teacher to filter through to the mind of an aspiring child; but, upon the whole, it is certain beyond controversy that the success of the teacher in teaching, and of the pupil in learning, will depend upon the intellectual equipment of the teacher.

To put literature into a course of study quite irrespective of the teacher's personal appreciation of literary values—to say nothing of accurate discrimination as to the facts—is to go at the matter from the wrong end. To enact that at a given date all the grades of a certain city shall have nature study is to invite confusion and distraction. It would be comic (if it were not tragic) to suppose that all that is required to make music and drawing a part of the course of study is to have the school board legislate that a certain amount of the time of the pupil, covering a certain prescribed ground, shall be given to work with pencil and paper, and to musical exercises. There is no magic by which these things can pass over from the printed page of the school manual to the child's consciousness. If the teacher has no standard of value in relation to them, no intimate personal reponse of feeling to them, no conception of the methods of art which alone bring the child to a corresponding intellectual and emotional attitude, these studies will remain what precisely they so often are — passing recreations, modes of showing off, or exercises in technique.

The special teacher has arisen because of the recognition of the inadequate preparation of the average teacher to get the best results with these newer subjects. Special teaching, however, shifts rather than solves the problem. As already indicated, the question is a twofold one. It is a question, not only of *what* is known, but of *how* it is known. The special instructor in nature study or art may have a better command of the what — of the actual material to be taught — but be deficient in the consciousness of the relations borne by that particular subject to other forms of experience in the child, and, therefore, to his own personal growth. When this is the case we exchange King Log for King Stork. We exchange an ignorant and superficial teaching for a vigorous but one-sided, because over-specialized, mode of instruction. The special teacher in manual training or what not, having no philosophy of education—having, that is, no view of the whole of which his own subject is a part—isolates that study and works it out wholly in terms of itself. His beginning and his end, as well as the intermediate materials and methods, fall within manual training. This may give technical facility, but it is not (save incidentally) education.

This is not an attack upon special or departmental teaching. On the contrary, I have just pointed out that this mode of teaching has arisen absolutely in response to the demands of the situation. Since our present teachers are so largely an outcome of the older education, the so-called all-around teacher is for the most part a myth. Moreover, it is a mistake to suppose that we can secure the all-around teacher merely by instructing him in a larger number of branches. In the first place, human capacity is limited. The person whose interests and powers are all-around is not as a rule teaching in grade schools. He is at the head of the great scientific, industrial, and political enterprises of civilization. But granted that the average teacher could master ten distinct studies as well as five, it still remains true that without intellectual organization, without definite insight into the relation of these studies to one another and to the whole of life, without ability to present them to the child from the standpoint of such insight, we simply add an overburdened and confused teacher to the overburdened and confused child. In a word, to make the teaching in the newer studies thoroughly effective, whether by specialists or by the all-around teacher, there must, in addition to knowledge of the particular branch, be sanity, steadiness, and system in the mental attitude of the instructor. It is folly to suppose that we can carry on the education of the child apart from the education of the teacher.

If I were to touch upon certain other matters fundamentally connected with the problem of securing the teachers who make the nominal course of study a reality, I should be started upon an almost endless road. However, we must not pass on without at least noticing that the question is one of political, as well as of intellectual organization. An adequate view of the whole situation would take into account the general social condition upon which depends the actual supplying of teachers to the schoolroom. The education of the candidate, of the would-be teacher, might be precisely that outlined above, and yet it would remain, to a large extent, inoperative, if the appointment of school-teachers was at the mercy of personal intrigue, political bargaining, and the effort of some individual or class to get power in the community through manipulation of patronage. It is sentimental to suppose that any large and decisive reform in the course of study can take place as long as such agencies influence what actually comes in a living way to the life of the child.

Nor in a more comprehensive view could we be entirely silent upon the need of commercial as well as political reform. Publishing companies affect not only the text-books and apparatus, the garb with which the curriculum clothes itself, but also and that directly the course of study itself. New studies are introduced because some pushing firm, by a happy coincidence, has exactly the books which are needed to make that study successful. Old studies which should be entirely displaced (if there be any logic in the introduction of the new one) are retained because there is a vested interest behind them. Happy is the large school system which is free from the congestion and distraction arising from just such causes as these. And yet there are those who discuss the relative merits of what they are pleased to call old and new education as if it were purely an abstract and intellectual matter.

But we cannot enter upon these larger phases. It is enough if we recognize the typical signs indicating the impossibility of separating either the theoretical discussion of the course of study or the problem of its practical efficiency from intellectual and social conditions which at first sight are far removed; it is enough if we recognize that the question of the course of study is a question in the organization of knowledge, in the organization of life, in the organization of society. And, for more immediate purposes, it is enough to recognize that certain conditions imbedded in the present scheme of school administration affect so profoundly results reached by the newer studies, by manual training, art and nature study, that it is absurd to discuss the the value or lack of value of the latter, without taking these considerations into account. I recur to my original proposition: that these studies are not having their own career, are not exhibiting their own powers, but are hampered and compromised by a school of machinery originated and developed with reference to quite different ends and aims. The real conflict is not between a certain group of studies, the three R's, those having to do with the symbols and tools of intellectual life, and other studies representing the personal development of the child, but between our professed ends and the means we are using to realize these ends.

The popular assumption, however, is to the contrary. It is still the common belief (and not merely in popular thought, but among those who profess to speak with authority) that the two groups of studies are definitely opposed to each other in their aims and methods, in the mental attitude demanded from the child, in the kind of work called for from the instructor. It is assumed that we have a conflict between one group of studies dealing only with the forms and symbols of knowledge, studies to be mastered by mechanical drill, and between those that appeal to the vital concerns of child life and afford present satisfaction. This assumed opposition has been so clearly stated in a recent educational document that I may be pardoned quoting at length :

In regard to education we may divide the faculties into two classes — the doing faculties and the thinking faculties. By the doing faculties I mean those mechanical habits which are essential to the acquisition of knowledge, and are pure arts, such as the art of reading; that of performing arithmetical operations with rapidity and correctness; that of expressing thoughts in legible characters, and in words of grammatical arrangement. These arts can only be acquired by laborious drilling on the part of the teacher, and labor on the part of the pupil. They require little instruction, but repetition until they are performed with ease and almost pleasure. To neglect to impart these habits is to do a great injury to the child; nothing should be substituted for them, though instruction in other branches which require more thought and less art may be mingled as recreations with them.

I have never seen so condensed and comprehensive a statement of the incompatibility of aims and method for both teacher and pupil as is given here. On one side we have "doing faculties," by which is meant powers of pure external efficiency. These find their expression in what are termed "arts," which is interpreted to mean purely mechanical habits — sheer routine facility. These are acquired by continued drill on the part of the teacher, and continued laborious repetition on the part of the child. Thought is not required in the process, nor is the result "instruction"—that is, a real building up of the mind; the outcome is simply command of powers, of value not in themselves, but as tools of further knowledge, as "essential to the acquisition of knowledge." The scheme of contrasting studies is not so well developed. It is made clear, however, that they appeal to thought, not to mechanical habits, and that they proceed by instruction, not by drill. It is further implied that their

exercise is attended not so much with labor as
with pleasure on the part of the child—which
may be interpreted to mean that they have a
present value in the life of the child, and are
not mere instrumentalities of remoter acquisition. ? The situation as regards school work
is contained in the proposition that the mechanical facilities based upon sheer drill and
laborious repetition must make up the bulk of
the elementary education, while the studies
which involve thought, the furnishing of the
mind itself, and result in a direct expansion of
life, "may be mingled as recreations." They
may be permitted, in other words, in the
schoolroom as an occasional relief from the
laborious drill of the more important studies.

Here is the dividing wall. The wall has
been somewhat undermined; breaches have
been worn in it; it has, as it were, been bodily
pushed along until the studies of thought, of
instruction and of present satisfaction occupy
a greater bulk of school time and work. But
the wall is still there. The mechanical habits
that are essential to the acquisition of knowledge, the art of reading, of performing arithmetical operations and of expressing thought
legibly and grammatically, are still the serious
business of the schoolroom. Nature study,
manual training, music, and art are incidents

introduced because of the "interests" they
provide, because they appeal to ability to think.
arouse general intelligence, and add to the
fund of information. A house divided against
itself cannot stand. If the results of our present system are not altogether and always sat-
isfactory, shall we engage in crimination and
recrimination—setting the old studies against
the new and the new against the old—or
shall we hold responsible the organization, or
lack of organization, intellectual and adminis
trative, in the school system itself? If the
old bottles will not hold the new wine, it is
conceivable that we should blame neither the
bottles nor the wine, but conditions which
have brought the two into mechanical and
external connection.

If my remarks in dwelling upon the split
and contradiction in the present situation appear to be unnecessarily gloomy, it should be
remembered that this view is optimism itself
as compared with the theory which holds that
the two groups of studies are radically opposed to each other in their ends, results, and
methods. Such a theory holds that there is a
fundamental contradiction between the present
and the future needs of the child, between
what his life requires as immediate nutritive
material and what it needs as preparation for

the future. It assumes a fundamental conflict between that which nourishes the spirit of the child and that which affords the instrumentalities of intellectual acquisition. It proclaims a fundamental opposition to exist in the mental activity between the methods of acquisition of skill, and the methods of development. The practical consequences are as disastrous as the logical split is complete. If the opposition be an intrinsic one, then the present conflict and confusion in the school-room are permanent and not transitory. We shall be forever oscillating between extremes: now lending ourselves with enthusiasm to the introduction of art and music and manual training, because they give vitality to the school-work and relief to the child; now querulously complaining of the evil results reached, and insisting with all positiveness upon the return of good old days when reading, writing, spelling, and arithmetic were adequately taught. Since by the theory there is no possibility of an organic connection, of co-operative relation, between the two types of study, the relative position of each in the curriculum must be decided from arbitrary and external grounds; by the wish and zeal of some strong man, or by the pressure of temporary popular sentiment. At the best we get only a compromise; at the worst we get a maximum of routine with a halo of sentiment thrown about it, or a great wish-wash of superficiality covering up the residuum of grind.

As compared with such a view, the conception that the conflict is not inherent in the studies themselves, but arises from maladjustment of school conditions, from survival of a mode of educational administration calculated for different ends from those now confronting us, is encouragement itself. The problem becomes first an intellectual and then a practical one. Intellectually what is needed is a philosophy of organization; a view of the organic unity of the educative process and educative material, and of the place occupied in this whole by each of its own parts. We need to know just what reading and writing and number do for the present life of the child, and how they do it. We need to know what the method of mind is which underlies subject-matter in cooking, shop-work and nature study, so that they may become effective for discipline, and not mere sources of present satisfaction and mere agencies of relief—so that they too may become as definitely modes of effective preparation for the needs of society as ever reading, writing, and arithmetic have been.

With our minds possessed by a sane and
coherent view of the whole situation, we may
attempt such a gradual, yet positive modification of existing procedure as will enable us
to turn theory into practice. Let us not be
too precipitate, however, in demanding light
upon just what to do next. We should re-
member that there are times when the most
practical thing is to face the *intellectual* problem, and to get a clear and comprehensive
survey of the theoretical factors involved. The
existing situation, with all its vagueness and
all its confusion, will nevertheless indicate
plenty of points of leverage, plenty of intelligent ways of straightening things out, to one
who approaches it with any clear conviction
of the ends he wishes to reach, and of the
obstacles in the way. An enlightenment of
vision is the prerequisite of efficiency in conduct. The conservative may devote himself
to the place of reading and writing and arithmetic in the curriculum so that they shall
vitally connect with the present needs of the
child's life, and afford the satisfaction that
always comes with the fulfilment, the expression, of present power. The reformer may
attack the problem, not at large and all over
the entire field, but at the most promising
point, whether it be art or manual training or

nature study, and concentrate all his efforts
upon educating alike the community, the
teacher and the child into the knowledge of
fundamental values for individual mind and
for community life embodied in that study.
Both conservative and reformer can devote
themselves to the problem of the better education of the teacher, and of doing away with
the hindrances to placing the right teacher
in the schoolroom; and to the hindrances
to continued growth after he is placed there.
The American people believe in education
above all else, and when the educators have
come to some agreement as to what education
is, the community will not be slow in placing
at their disposal the equipment and resources
necessary to make their ideal a reality.

In closing let me say that I have intention-
ally emphasized the obstacles to further progress, rather than congratulated ourselves upon
the progress already made. The anomaly and
confusion have, after all, been of some use.
In some respects the blind conflict of the last
two generations of educational history has
been a better way of changing the conditions
than would have been some wholesale and *a
priori* rearrangement. The forms of genuine
growth always come slowly. The struggle of
the newer studies to get a foothold in the cur-

riculum, with all the attendant confusion, is an experiment carried out on a large scale ; an experiment in natural selection, of the survival of the fit in educational forms.

Yet there must come a time when blind experimentation is to give way to something more directed. The struggle should bring out the factors in the problem so that we can go more intelligently to work in its solution. The period of blind striving, of empirical adjustment, trying now this and now that, making this or that combination because it is feasible for the time being, of advancing here and retreating there, of giving headway now to the instinct of progress and now to the habit of inertia, should find an outcome in some illumination of vision, in some clearer revelation of the realities of the situation. It is uneconomical to prolong the period of conflict between incompatible tendencies. It makes for intellectual hypocrisy to suppose that we are doing what we are not doing. It weakens the nerve of judgment and the fiber of action to submit to conditions which prevent the realization of aims to which we profess ourselves to be devoted.

My topic is the elementary educational situation. In a somewhat more limited and precise view than I have previously taken of

the situation, I believe we are now nearing
the close of the time of tentative, blind, empirical experimentation; that we are close to
the opportunity of planning our work on the
basis of a coherent philosophy of experience
and a philosophy of the relation of school
studies to that experience; that we can accordingly take up steadily and wisely the effort
of changing school conditions so as to make
real the aims that command the assent of our
intelligence and the support of our moral enthusiasm.

II. AS CONCERNS SECONDARY EDUCATION.

I SHOULD feel hesitant indeed to come before a body of teachers, engaged in the practical work of teaching, and appear to instruct them regarding the solution of the difficult problems which face them. My task is a more grateful one. It is mine simply to formulate and arrange the difficulties which the current state of discussion shows teachers already to have felt. Those concerned with secondary school work have realized that their energies must be peculiarly concentrated at certain points; they have found that some problems are so urgent that they must be met and wrestled with. I have tried in the accompanying syllabus to gather together these practical problems and to arrange them in such form as to show their connections with one another; and by this classification to indicate what seemed to me the roots of the difficulty.

I. *Problems relating to the articulation of the secondary school in the educational system.*

   1. Adjustment to the grades.

      a) Dropping out of pupils : extent and causes.

      b) Different sorts of preparation of teachers ; methods of rectifying, etc.

c) Abrupt change of ideals and methods of teaching and discipline.

d) Introduction of traditional high-school studies into the upper grades; the science course, etc.

2. Adjustment to college.

a) Modes of entering college; examination, certification, etc.

b) Varieties of entrance requirements.

c) Different problems of public and private high schools.

d) Coaching for specific results *vs.* training and method.

II. *Problems relating to the adjustment of preparation for college to preparation for other pursuits in life.*

1. Is it true that the same education gives the best preparation for both?

2. If so, which shall be taken as the standard for measuring the character of the other?

3. If not so, by what principles and along what lines shall the work be differentiated?

4. If not so, shall specialized or definite preparation be made for other future callings as well as for the college student?

III. *The adjustment of work to the individual.*

1. The nature and limits of the elective principle as applied to particular subjects, and to courses and groups of subjects.

2. Acquaintance with the history, environment, and capacity of individuals with reference to assisting in the selection of vocation.

3. Does the period of adolescence present such peculiarities as to call for marked modifications of present secondary work?

IV. *Problems arising from social phases of secondary-school work.*

    1. The educational utilization of social organizations: debating, musical, dramatic clubs; athletics.

    2. School discipline and government in their social aspects.

    3. Relations to the community: the school as a social center.

V. *Preceding problems as affecting the curriculum: conflict of studies and groups of studies.*

    1. The older problem: adjustment of the respective claims of ancient and modern languages, of language and science, of history and social science, civics, economics, etc., of English literature and composition.

    2. The newer problem:

        a) The place of manual training and technological work.

        b) The place of fine art.

        c) Commercial studies.

In what I have to say this morning, I shall make no attempt to go over these points one by one. I shall rather try to set clearly and briefly before you the reasons which have led me to adopt the classification presented. This will take me into a discussion of the historic and social facts which lie back of the problems, and in the light of which alone I believe these problems can be attacked and solved. If it seems unnecessarily remote to approach school problems through a presentation of what may appear to be simply a form

of social philosophy, there is yet practical encouragement in recognizing that exactly the
same forces which have thrust these questions
into the forefront of school practice, are also
operative to solve them. For problems do
not arise arbitrarily. They come from causes,
and from causes which are imbedded in the
very structure of the school system — yes,
even beyond that, in the structure of society
itself. It is for this reason that mere changes
in the mechanics of the school system, whether in administration or in the externals of subject-matter, turn out mere temporary devices.
Sometimes, when one has made a delicate or
elaborate arrangement which seems to him
exactly calculated to obviate the difficulties of
the situation, one is tempted to accuse his
generation as stiff-necked when the scheme
does not take — when it does not spread;
when, in the language of the biologist, it is
not selected. The explanation, however, is
not in the hard-heartedness or intellectual
blindness of others, but in the fact that any
adjustment which really and permanently suc-
ceeds within the school walls, must reach out
and be an adjustment of forces in the social
environment.

A slight amount of social philosophy and
social insight reveals two principles continu-

ously at work in all human institutions: one
is toward specialization and consequent isolation, the other toward connection and interaction.   In the life of the nation we see first a
movement toward separation, toward marking
off our own life as a people as definitely as
possible to avoid its submergence, to secure
for it an individuality of its own.   Commer-
cially we pursue a policy of protection; in
international relations one of having to do as
little as possible with other nationalities. That
tendency exhausts itself and the pendulum
swings in another direction.   Reciprocity, the
broadening of our business life through in-
creased contacts and wider exchange, becomes
the commercial watchword.   Expansion, taking our place in the sisterhood of nations,
making ourselves recognized as a world-power,
becomes the formula for international politics.
Science shows the same rhythm in its development.   A period of specialization—of relative
isolation—secures to each set of natural phenomena a chance to develop on its own account, without being lost in, or obscured by
generalities or a mass of details.   But the time
comes when the limit of movement in this
direction is reached, and it is necessary to
devote ourselves to tracing the threads of
connection which unite the different special-

ized branches into a coherent and consecutive whole. At present the most active sciences seem to be spelled with a hyphen; it is astro-physics, stereo-chemistry, psycho-physics, and so on.

This is not a movement of blind action and reaction. One tendency is the necessary completion of the other. A certain degree of isolation of detachment is required to secure the unhindered and mature development of any group of forces. It is necessary in order to master them in their practical workings. We have to divide to conquer. But when the proper degree of individualization is reached, we need to bring one thing to bear upon another in order to realize upon the benefits which may be derived from the period of iso-lation. The sole object of the separation is to serve as a means to the end of more effective interaction.

Now as to the bearings of this abstract piece of philosophy upon our school prob-lems. The school system is a historic evo-lution. It has a tradition and a movement of its own. Its roots run back into the past and may be traced through the strata of the successive centuries. It has an independence, a dignity of its own comparable to that of any other institution. In this twenty-five-hundred-year-old development it has, of necessity, taken on its individuality at the expense of a certain isolation. Only through this isolation has it been disentangled from absorption in other institutions : the family, government, the church, and so on. This detachment has been a necessity in order that it might become a true division of labor and thus perform most efficiently the service required of it.

But there are disadvantages as well as advantages. Attention has come to be concentrated upon the affairs of the school system as if they concerned simply the system itself, and had only a very indirect reference to other social institutions. The school-teacher often resents reference to outside contacts and considerations as if they were indeed outside— simply interferences. There can be no doubt that in the last two centuries much more thought and energy have been devoted to shaping the school system into an effective mechanism within itself than to securing its due interaction with family life, the church, commerce, or political institutions.

But, having secured this fairly adequate and efficient machine, the question which is coming more and more to the front is : what shall we do with it ? How shall we secure from it the services, the fruits, which alone justify the expense of money, time, and thought in building up the machine?

It is at this point that particular conflicts and problems begin to show themselves. The contemporary demands—the demands that are made in the attempt to secure the proper interaction of the school—are one thing; the demands that arise out of the working of the school system considered as an independent historical institution are another. Every teacher has to work at detailed problems which arise out of this conflict, whether he is aware of its existence or not, and is he harassed by friction that arises in the conflict of these two great social forces. Men divide along these lines. We find one group instinctively rather than consciously ranging themselves about the maintenance of the existing school system, and holding that reforms are to be made along the line of improvement in its present workings. Others are clamorous for more radical changes—the changes which will better adapt the school to contemporary social needs. Needless to say, each represents a necessary and essential factor in the situation, because each stands for the working of a force which cannot be eliminated.

Let me now try to show how, out of this profound social conflict and necessity of social

adjustment, the particular problems arise which
I have arranged under five heads in the accompanying syllabus. Our first concern is with
the articulation of the high school into the
entire educational system. The high school
looks towards the grades on one side and
toward the college on the other. What are
the historic influences which have shaped this
intermediate position, and placed peculiar difficulties and responsibilities upon the secondary school? Briefly put, it is that the
elementary school and the college represent
distinctly different forces and traditions on
the historic side. The elementary school is an
outgrowth of the democratic movement in its
ethical aspects. Prior to the latter half of the
eighteenth century the elementary school was
hardly more than a wooden device for instructing little children of the lower classes in some
of the utilities of their future callings—the
mere rudiments of reading, writing, and number. The democratic upheaval took shape
not merely in a demand for political equality,
but in a more profound aspiration towards an
equality of intellectual and moral opportunity
and development. The significance of such an
educational writer as Rousseau is not measured
by any particular improvement he suggested,
or by any particular extravagances he indulged

himself in. His is a voice struggling to ex-
press the necessity of a thoroughgoing revolution of elementary education to make it a
factor in the intellectual and moral development of all—not a mere device for teaching
the use of certain practical tools to those sec-
tions of society before whose development a
stone wall was placed. What Rousseau as a
writer was to the emotions of the France of
his day, Horace Mann as a doer was to the
practical situation of the United States in his
time. He stood, and stood most effectively,
for letting the democratic spirit, in all of its
ethical significance, into the common elementary schools, and for such a complete reorganization of these schools as would make
them the most serviceable possible instruments of human development.

In spite of all the influences which are continually operative to limit the scope and range
of elementary education, in spite of the influences which would bring back a reversion
to the type of the limited utilitarian school
of the seventeenth century, that part of the
school system which stands underneath the
high school represents this broad democratic
movement. To a certain extent, and in many
of its phases, the high school is an outgrowth
of exactly the same impulse. It has the same

history and stands for the same ideals; but only in part. It has also been profoundly shaped by influences having another origin. It represents also the tradition of the learned class. It maintains the tradition of higher culture as a distinct possession of a certain class of society. It embodies the aristocratic ideal. If we cast our eyes back over history, we do not find its full meaning summed up in the democratic movement of which I have just spoken. We find the culture of the ancient world coming down to us by a distinct channel. We find the wisdom and enlightenment of the past conserved and handed on by a distinct class located almost entirely in the colleges, and in the higher academies which are to all intents and purposes the outgrowth of the colleges. We find that our high school has been quite as persistently molded and directed through the agencies which have been concerned with keeping alive and passing on the treasure of learning, as through the democratic influences which have surged up from below. The existing high school, in a word, is a product of the meeting of these two forces, and upon it more than upon any other part of the school system is placed the responsibility of making an adjustment.

I do not mention the tradition of learning

kept up in the universities of the Middle Ages
and the higher schools of the Renaissance, and
refer to it as aristocratic for the sake of dis-
paraging it. Eternal vigilance is the price of
liberty, and eternal care and nurture are the
price of maintaining the precious conquest of
the past — of preventing a relapse into Philis-
tinism, that combination of superficial enlightenment and dogmatic crudity. If it were not
for the work of an aristocracy in the past,
there would be but little worth conferring upon
the democracy of today.

There are not in reality two problems of
articulation for the high school — one as regards the grades and the other as regards the
college. There is at bottom but one problem
— that of adjusting the demand for an adequate training of the masses of mankind to
the conservation and use of that higher learning which is the primary and essential concern of a smaller number — of a minority. Of
course, elementary school and college alike
are effected by the same problem. Part of
the work of the grades today is precisely the
enrichment of its traditional meager and materialistic curriculum with something of that
spirit and wealth of intelligence that are the
product of the higher schools. And one of
the problems of the college is precisely to

make its store of learning more available to the masses, make it count for more in the everyday life.

But the high school is the connecting link, and it must bear the brunt. Unless I am a false prophet, we shall soon see the same thoughtful attention which for the past fifteen years has characterized discussion of the relation of high school and college, speedily transferring itself over to the problem of a more organic and vital relation between the high school and the grades. The solution of this problem is important in order that the democratic movement may not be abortively arrested—in order that it may have its full sweep. But it is equally important, for the sake of the college, and in the interests of higher learning. The arbitrary hiatus which exists at present reacts as unfavorably in one direction as in the other.

First, it limits the constituency of the college; it lessens the actual numbers of those who are awakened to the opportunities before them, and directed towards the college doors. Secondly, it restricts the sphere of those who sympathetically and vicariously feel the influence of the college, and are thus led to feel that what concerns the welfare of the college is of direct concern to them. The attitude of the mass of the people today towards the college is one of curiosity displaying itself from afar rather than of immediate interest. Indeed, it sometimes would seem that only athletic exhibitions form a direct line of connection between the college and the average community life. In the third place it tends to erect dams which prevent the stream of teachers flowing from the college walls from seeking or finding congenial service in the grades, and thereby tends automatically to perpetuate whatever narrowness of horizon or paucity of resource is characteristic of the elementary school. Fourth, it operates to isolate the college in its working relations to life, and thereby to hinder it from rendering its normal service to society.

I pass on now to the second main line of problems — those having to do with preparation for college on one side, and for life on the other. Ultimately this is not a different problem, but simply another outgrowth of the same question. A few years ago a happy formula was current: the proposition that the best preparation for college was also the best preparation for life. The formula was such a happy one that if formulæ ever really disposed of any practical difficulty, there would be no longer any problem to discuss. But I seem to ob-

serve that this proposition is not heard so frequently as formerly; and indeed, that since it
was uttered things seem to be taking their own
course much as before.

The inefficiency of the formula lies in its am-
biguity. It throws no light on the fundamental problem of Which is Which? Is it preparation for college which sets the standard for
preparation for life, or is it preparation for life
which affords the proper criterion of adequate
preparation for college? Is the high-school
course to be planned primarily with reference
to meeting the needs of those who go to college, on the assumption that this will also
serve best the needs of those who go into
other callings in life? Or, shall the high
school devote its energies to preparing all its
members for life in more comprehensive sense,
and permit the college to select its entrance
requirements on the basis of work thus done?

I shall not attempt to solve this problem,
and for a very good reason. I believe that
there are forces inherent in the situation itself
which are working out an inevitable solution.
Every step in the more rational development
of both high school and college, without any
reference to their relationships to each other
bring the two more closely together. I am
optimistic enough to believe that we are much

nearer a solution of this vexed question than we generally dare believe. Quite independent of any question of entrance requirements, or of high-school preparation, the college is undergoing a very marked development, and even transformation, on its own account. I refer to such developments within the college course as the introduction not only of the Ph. B. and B. S. courses side by side with the older classical courses, but also to the forward movement in the direction of a specific group of commercial and social studies; and to the tendency of all universities of broad scope to maintain technological schools. I refer also to the tendency to adapt the college work more and more to preparation for specific vocations in life. Practically all the larger colleges of the country now have a definite arrangement by which at least one year of the undergraduate course counts equally in the professional course. of law, medicine, or divinity as the case may be. Now, when these two movements have reached their fruition, and the high school has worked out on its own account the broadening of its own curriculum, I believe we shall find that the high school and the college have arrived at a common point. The college course will be so broad and varied that it will be entirely feasible to take any judicious group of studies from any well organized and well managed high school, and accept them as preparation for college. It has been the narrowness of the traditional college curriculum on one side, and the inadequacy of the content of high-school work on the other, which have caused a large part of our mutual embarrassments.

I must run rapidly over the problems referred to under my third and fourth main heads—those having to do with adjustment to individual needs, and to the social uses of the school. I take it that these illustrate just the same general principle we have been already discussing. The school has a tradition not only regarding its position in the educational system as a whole, and not only as regards its proper curriculum, but also as regards the methods and ideals of discipline and administration in relation to its students.

There can be no doubt that many of these traditions are out of alignment with the general trend of events outside the school walls—that in some cases the discrepancy is so great that the high-school tradition cuts abruptly across this outside stream. One of these influences is found in the tendency equally marked in the family, church, and state, to relax the bonds of purely external authority, to give more play to individual powers, to require of the individual more personal initiative, and to exact of him a more personal accountability. There may be difference of opinion as to the degree in which the school should yield to this tendency, or should strive to counteract it, or should endeavor to utilize and direct it. There can be no difference of opinion, however, as to the necessity of a more persistent and adequate study of the individual as regards his history, environment, predominant tastes and capacities, and special needs — and please note that I say needs as well as tastes. I do not think there can be any difference of opinion as to the necessity of a more careful study of the effect of particular school studies upon the normal growth of the individual, and of the means by which they shall be made a more effective means of connection between the present powers of the individual, and his future career. Just the limits of this principle, and its bearings upon such problems as the introduction of electives, I shall not take up. We have no time for a detailed discussion of these disputed points. As I have just indicated, however, I do not see how there can be dispute as to the fact that the individual has assumed such a position as to require more positive consideration and attention as an individual, and a correspondingly different mode of treatment.

I cannot leave the topic, however, without stating that here also I believe the ultimate solution will be found, not along the line of mechanical devices as to election or non-election, but rather through the more continued and serious study of the individual in both his psychological make-up and his social relations.

I have reserved the group of problems bearing upon the formation of a curriculum until the last. From the practical side, however, we probably find here the problems which confront the average teacher most urgently and persistently. This I take it is because all the other influences impinge at this point. The problem of just what time is to be given respectively to mathematics, and classics, and modern languages, and history, and English, and the sciences — physical, biological — is one the high-school teacher has always with him. To adjust the respective claims of the different studies and get a result which is at once harmonious and workable, is a task which almost defies human capacity. The problem, however, is not a separate problem. It is so pressing just because it is at this point that all the other forces meet. The adjustment of studies, and courses of study, is the ground upon which the practical solution and working adjustment of all other problems must be sought and

found. It is as an effect of other deep lying
and far-reaching historic and social causes
that the conflict of studies is to be treated.

There is one matter constantly accompanying any practical problem which at first sight
is extremely discouraging. Before we get
our older problems worked out to any degree of satisfaction, new and greater problems are upon us, threatening to overwhelm
us. Such is the present educational situation.
It would seem as if the question of adjusting the conflicts already referred to, which
have so taxed the time and energy of high-
school teachers for the past generation, were
quite enough. But no; before we have arrived at anything approaching consensus of
opinion, the larger city schools at least find
the conflict raging in a new spot — still other
studies and lines of study are demanding recognition. We have the uprearing of the commercial high school; of the manual-training
high school.

At first the difficulty of the problem was
avoided or evaded, because distinct and separate high schools were erected to meet these
purposes. The current now seems to be in
the other direction. A generation ago it was
practically necessary to isolate the manual-
training course of study in order that it

might receive due attention, and be worked out under fairly favorable influences. Fifteen years ago the same was essentially true of the commercial courses. Now, however, there are many signs of the times indicating that the situation is ripe for interaction —the problem is now the introduction of manual-training and commercial courses as integral and organic parts of a city high school. Demands are also made for the introduction of more work in the line of fine art, drawing, music, and the application of design to industry; and for the introduction of a larger number of specifically sociological studies—this independent of those studies which naturally form a part of the so-called commercial course.

At first sight, as just intimated, the introduction of these new difficulties before we are half way through our old ones, is exceedingly distressing. But more than once the longest way around has proved the shortest way home. When new problems emerge, it must mean, after all, that certain essential conditions of the old problem had been ignored, and consequently that any solution reached simply in terms of the recognized factors would have been partial and temporary. I am inclined to think that in the present case the introduction of these new problems will

ultimately prove enlightening rather than con-
fusing. They serve to generalize the older
problems, and to make their factors stand out
in clearer relief.

In the future it is going to be less and less a
matter of worrying over the respective merits of
the ancient and modern languages; or of the inherent values of scientific *vs.* humanistic study,
and more a question of discovering and ob-
serving certain broader lines of cleavage,
which affect equally the disposition and power
of the individual, and the social callings for
which education ought to prepare the individual. It will be, in my judgment, less and less
a question of piecing together certain studies
in a more or less mechanical way in order to
make out a so-called course of study running
through a certain number of years; and more
and more a question of grouping studies together according to their natural mutual affini-
ties and reinforcements for the securing of
certain well-marked ends.

For this reason I welcome the introduction
into the arena of discussion, of the question
of providing courses in commerce and sociology, in the fine and applied arts, and in
technological training. I think henceforth
certain fundamental issues will stand out more
clearly and have to be met upon a wider

basis and dealt with on a wider scale. As I see the matter, this change will require the concentration of attention upon these two points: first, what groups of studies will most serviceably recognize the typical divisions of labor, the typical callings in society, callings which are absolutely indispensable to the spiritual as well as to the material ends of society; and, secondly, not to do detriment to the real culture of the individual, or, if this seems too negative a statement, to secure for him the full use and control of his own powers. From this point of view, I think that certain of the problems just referred to, as, for instance, the conflict of language and science, will be put in a new perspective, will be capable of approach from a different angle; and that because of this new approach many of the knotty problems which have embarrassed us in the past will disappear.

Permit me to repeat in a somewhat more explicit way the benefits which I expect to flow from the expansion of the regular high school in making room for commercial, manual, and æsthetic studies. In the first place, it will provide for the recognition and the representation of all the typical occupations that are found in society. Thus it will make the working relationship between the secondary

school and life a free and all around one. It
will complete the circuit—it will round out
the present series of segmental arcs into a
whole. Now this fact will put all the school
studies in a new light. They can be looked at
in the place they normally occupy in the whole
circle of human activities. As long as social
values and aims are only partially represented
in the school, it is not possible to employ the
standard of social value in a complete way. A
continual angle of refraction and distortion is
introduced in viewing existing studies, through
the fact that they are looked at from an artifi-
cial standpoint. Even those studies which are
popularly regarded as preparing distinctively
for life rather than for college cannot get
their full meaning, cannot be judged correctly,
until the life for which they are said to be a
preparation receives a fuller and more balanced representation in the school. While, on
the other hand, the more scholastic studies, if
I may use the expression, cannot relate themselves properly so long as the branches which
give them their ultimate *raison d'être* and
sphere of application in the whole of life are
non-existent in the curriculum.

For a certain type of mind algebra and
geometry are their own justification. They
appeal to such students for the intellectual

satisfaction they supply, and as preparation
for the play of the intellect in further studies.
But to another type of mind these studies are
relatively dead and meaningless until sur-
rounded with a context of obvious bearings—
such as furnished in manual-training studies.
The latter, however, are rendered unduly utilitarian and narrow when isolated. Just as in
life the technological pursuits reach out and
affect society on all sides, so in the school
corresponding studies need to be imbedded
in a broad and deep matrix.

In the second place, as previously suggested,
the explanation of the high school simplifies
instead of complicates the college preparatory
problem. This is because the college is going
through an analogous evolution in the introduction of similar lines of work. It is ex-
panding in technological and commercial
directions. To be sure, the branch of fine and
applied arts is still practically omitted; it is
left to the tender mercies of over-specialized
and more or less mercenary institutions—
schools where these things are taught more or
less as trades, and for the sake of making
money. But the same influences which have
already rescued medical and commercial edu-
tion from similar conditions, and have brought
to bear upon them the wider outlook and more

expert method of the university, will in time make themselves also felt as regards the teaching of art.

Thirdly, the wider high school relieves many of the difficulties in the adequate treatment of the individual as an individual. It brings the individual into a wider sphere of contacts, and thus makes it possible to test him and his capacity more thoroughly. It makes it possible to get at and remedy his weak points by balancing more evenly the influences that play upon him. In my judgment many of the problems now dealt with under the general head of election *vs.* prescription can be got at more correctly and handled more efficiently from the standpoint of the elastic *vs.* the rigid curriculum — and elasticity can be had only where there is breadth. The need is not so much an appeal to the untried and more or less capricious choice of the individual as for a region of opportunities large enough and balanced enough to meet the individual on his every side, and provide for him that which is necessary to arouse and direct.

Finally, the objection usually urged to the broader high school is, when rightly considered, the strongest argument for its existence. I mean the objection that the introduction of manual training and commercial studies is a cowardly surrender on the part of liberal culture of the training of the man as a man, to utilitarian demands for specialized adaptation to narrow callings. There is nothing in any one study or any one calling which makes it in and of itself low or meanly practical. It is all a question of its isolation or of its setting. It is not the mere syntactical structure or etymological content of the Latin language which has made it for centuries such an unrivaled educational instrument. There are dialects of semi-barbarous tribes which in intricacy of sentential structure and delicacy of relationship, are quite equal to Latin in this respect. It is the context of the Latin language, the wealth of association and suggestion belonging to it from its position in the history of human civilization that freight it with such meaning.

Now the callings that are represented by manual training and commercial studies are absolutely indispensable to human life. They afford the most permanent and persistent occupations of the great majority of human kind. They present man with his most perplexing problems; they stimulate him to the most strenuous putting forth of effort. To indict a whole nation were a grateful task compared with labeling such occupations as low or narrow—lacking in all that makes for training and culture. The professed and professional representative of "culture" may well hesitate to cast the first stone. It may be that it is nothing in these pursuits themselves which gives them utilitarian and materialistic quality, but rather the exclusive selfishness with which he has endeavored to hold on to and monopolize the fruits of the spirit.

And so with the corresponding studies in the high school. Isolated, they may be chargable with the defects of which they are accused. But they are convicted in this respect only because they have first been condemned to isolation. As representatives of serious and permanent interests of humanity, they possess an intrinsic dignity which it is the business of the educator to take account of. To ignore them, to deny them a rightful position in the educational circle, is to maintain within society that very cleft between so-called material and spiritual interests which it is the business of education to strive to overcome. These studies root themselves in science; they have their trunk in human history, and they flower in the worthiest and fairest forms of human service.

It is for these various reasons that I believe the introduction of the new problem of adjustment of studies will help instead of hinder the settlement of the older controversies. We have been trying for a long time to fix a curriculum upon a basis of certain vague and general educational ideals: information, utility, discipline, culture. I believe that much of our ill success has been due to the lack of any well-defined and controllable meaning attaching to these terms. The discussion remains necessarily in the region of mere opinion when the measuring rods are subject to change with the standpoint and wishes of the individual. Take any body of persons, however intelligent and however conscientious, and ask them to value and arrange studies from the standpoint of culture, discipline, and utility, and they will of necessity arrive at very different results, depending upon their own temperament and more or less accidental experience —and this none the less because of their intelligence and conscientiousness.

With the rounding out of the high school to meet all the needs of life, the standard changes. It ceases to be these vague abstractions. We get, relatively speaking, a scientific problem— that is a problem with definite data and definite methods of attack. We are no longer concerned with the abstract appraisal of studies by the measuring rod of culture or discipline. Our problem is rather to study the typical necessities of social life, and the actual nature of the individual in his specific needs and capacities. Our task is on one hand to select and adjust the studies with reference to the nature of the individual thus discovered; and on the other hand to order and group them so that they shall most definitely and systematically represent the chief lines of social endeavor and social achievement.

Difficult as these problems may be in practice, they are yet inherently capable of solution. It is a definite problem, a scientific problem, to discover what the nature of the individual is and what his best growth calls for. It is a definite problem, a scientific problem, to discover the typical vocations of society, and to find out what groupings of studies will be the most likely instruments to subserve these vocations. To dissipate the clouds of opinion, to restrict the influence of abstract and conceited argument; to stimulate the spirit of inquiry into actual fact, to further the control of the conduct of the school by the truths thus scientifically discovered—these are the benefits which we may anticipate with the advent of this problem of the wider high school.

III. AS CONCERNS THE COLLEGE.

THE elementary school is, by the necessity of the case, in closest contact with the wants of the people at large. It is the public-school, the common-school, system. It aims at universality in its range, at including all children. It has a universal basis, coming home to every citizen as a taxpayer. The higher institutions of learning are less under the control of immediate public opinion, with the ebb and flow of popular sentiment. They are set apart, as it were, under the control of specially selected leaders. They are dominated by a more continuous system of educational principle and policy. Their roots are in the past; they are the conservators of the wisdom, insight, and resources of bygone ages. While they may be part of the state system, yet they touch the average citizen in a much less direct way than does the elementary school. The secondary school is intermediate; it is between the upper and the nether millstone. On one side, it is subject to pressure from current public opinion; on the other, to the pressure of university tradition. While the public high school is more sensitive in the former direction, and the private academy more sensitive in the latter, neither one can be free from both influences.

The elementary school has both the advantages and the disadvantages of its more direct contact with public opinion. It is thereby more likely to respond promptly to what the people currently want. But, on the other hand, it is rendered liable to the fluctuations and confusions of the public's expression of its own needs. The higher institution has the advantages and the disadvantage of its greater remoteness, its greater isolation. The advantage is in the possibility of more definite leadership by those consistently trained in continuous educational standards and methods —freedom from the meaningless and arbitrary flux and reflux of public sentiment. The disadvantages are summed up in the unfavorable connotation of "academic," the suggestion of living in the past rather than the present, in the cloister rather than the world, in a region of abstraction rather than of practice.

The lower schools are more variable, and probably vary too easily and frequently as the various winds of public sentiment blow upon them. They are freighted with too little ballast. The traditional elementary school curriculum was so largely a formal thing, there was so little of substantial content in it,

that it could not offer much resistance to external pressure. There was also less ballast in
the matter of its teaching force, since the
standard of requirement in scholarship and
training was so much lower than that of the
higher schools. But this in no respect detracts
from their being the public, the common,
schools—that with which the interests of the
people are most closely and universally bound
up. It only emphasizes, after all, the necessity
of their being responsive to the needs of the
people, and not to traditions or conventions
from whatever source they arise.

The higher institutions are freighted with
a definite body of tradition. Their curriculum
represents the enduring experience and thought
of the centuries. They are the connecting
links binding us of today with the culture of
Greece and Rome and Mediæval Europe.
They are under the guidance of men who have
been subjected to uniform training, who have
been steeped in almost identical ideals, and
with whom teaching is a profession and not an
accident. In their method of administration
they are much more removed from public
opinion and sentiment than are the elementary
schools.

Does this mean, however, that the college
is relieved of the necessity of meeting public

needs, of acting with reference to social considerations ; or rather, that its problem, its function with reference to this need, is a peculiar and distinctive one ?   Our answer is unhesitatingly the latter. If the college derives more from the past, it is only that it may put more effectually the resources of the past at the disposition of the present. If it is more remote from immediate pressure of public demands, this should be regarded as imposing a duty, not as conferring an otiose privilege. It emphasizes the responsibility of steadying and clarifying the public consciousness, of rendering it less spasmodic, less vacillating, less confused; of imparting to it consistency and organization. The college has undertaken to maintain the continuity of culture. But culture should not be a protected industry, living at the expense of the freedom and completeness of present social communication and interaction. The sole reason for maintaining the continuity of culture is to make that culture operative in the conditions of modern life, of daily life, of political and industrial life, if you will.

It is comparatively easy to divorce these two functions. At one end of the scale we can erect the culture college; the college which, upon the whole, in its curriculum and methods ignores the demands of the present and insists upon the well-rounded and symmetrical education of the past — an education which is well-rounded simply because the insistent demands of the present are kept from breaking into it. At the other end of the scale is the distinctively professional technological school, which prepares specifically and definitely for the occupations of the present day; and which certainly is responding in consistent and obvious ways to current social needs and demands.

But, speaking for the higher institutions of learning as a whole, it is clear that both of these types of institutions solve the problem by unduly simplifying it. This is not to say that each has not its own place. It is only to say that that place is not the place of our higher institutions of learning taken in their entirety. Their problem is to join together what is here sundered, the culture factor (by which is meant acquaintance with the best that has been thought and said and done in the past) and the practical factor — or, more truly speaking, the social factor, the factor of adaptation to the present need.

But what, you may ask, is the working equivalent of this proposition? What effect would the attempt to carry it out have upon the existing college curriculum and method ? How does it bear, for example, upon the mooted question of the relation of the languages or the humanities to the sciences ? What bearing does it have upon the mooted question of the required *versus* the elective curriculum ? What bearing does it have upon the question of the method of instruction ? Shall it be dogmatic and disciplinary, so as to secure to the student the advantage of a stable point of view and a coherent body of material, or shall it be stimulating and liberating, aiming at ability to inquire, judge and act for one's self ?

The problem of the multiplication of studies, of the consequent congestion of the curriculum, and the conflict of various studies for a recognized place in the curriculum; the fact that one cannot get in without crowding something else out; the effort to arrange a compromise in various courses of study by throwing the entire burden of election upon the student so that he shall make out his own course of study — this problem is only a reflex of the lack of unity in the social activities themselves, and of the necessity of reaching more harmony, more system in our scheme of life. This multiplication of study is not primarily a product of the schools. The last hundred years has created a new world, has revealed a new universe, material and social. The educational problem is not a result of anything within our own conscious wish or intention, but of the conditions in the contemporary world.

Take, for illustration, the problem of the introduction and place of the sciences. I suppose all of us sometimes hear arguments whose implication is that a certain body of self-willed men invented the sciences, and are now, because of narrowness of culture, bent upon forcing them into prominence in the college curriculum. But it needs only to make this implication explicit to realize what a travesty it is. These sciences are the outcome of all that makes our modern life what it is. They are expressions of the agencies upon which the carrying on of our civilization is completely dependent. They did not grow out of professional, but of human, needs. They find their serious application in the schools only because they are everywhere having their serious application in life. There is no pressing industrial question that has not arisen in some new discovery regarding the forces of nature, and whose ultimate solution does not depend upon some further insight into the truths of nature—upon some scientific advance.

The revolution which is going on in industry
because of the advance of natural science, in
turn affects all professions and occupations.
It touches municipal government as well as
personal hygiene; it affects the calling of the
clergy as significantly, even if more indirectly,
as that of the lawyer. An intellectual and
social development of such scope cannot possibly take place and not throw our educational
curriculum into a state of distraction and un-
certainty.

When we are asked "Why not leave alone
all the new subjects not yet well organized
in themselves, and not well elaborated as
material for education; why not confine ourselves to the studies which have been taught
so long as to be organized for purposes of
instruction?"—when these questions are put
to us, we come upon a logical self-contradic-
tion and a practical impossibility.

The logical contradiction is found in the
fact that the new studies are not so isolated
from the old studies as to be lopped off in this
arbitrary way. In spite of confusion and conflict, the movement of the human mind is a
unity. The development of the new sciences
is not a mere addition of so much bulk of information to what went before. It represents
a profound modification and reconstruction of

all attained knowledge—a change in quality
and standpoint. The existing conflict between
the sciences and the humanities in the contemporary college curriculum· would not be
terminated by eliminating the sciences. Precisely the same conflict would at once reflect
itself within what is left over, the languages.
The scientific method has invaded this region
and claims it for its own. The lines would
soon be drawn between those who represent
the distinctively "scientific" aspects of language—phonology, philology, the strict historical development, the analytic determination of style, etc.—and those upholding the
banner of pure literary appreciation. The
point comes out more plainly by inquiring
what we are to do with the modern social and
historical sciences. No fact in controversy is
more recurrent (or more amusing) than that
while the contestants are struggling in the
dark, the center of the battle somehow mana·
ges to remove itself to another point; and
when the smoke clears away there is not only
a new battlefield, but an entirely new point at
issue. While the struggle between the classi-
cists and the scientists has been going on, a new
body of studies has been gradually making its
way, and is now reaching the point of conscious insistence upon its own claims. His-

tory, sociology, political science, and political economy may certainly claim to stand for the humanities. Quite as much as any linguistic phenomena, they represent fundamental values of human life. Yet they are the offspring of the scientific method. Apart from underlying biological conceptions, apart from the scientific conception of evolution, apart from that more intangible atmosphere which we call the scientific spirit, they would neither exist nor be making their way into the curriculum. The body of knowledge is indeed one; it is a spiritual organism. To attempt to chop off a member here and amputate an organ there is the veriest impossibility. The problem is not one of elimination, but of organization; of simplification not through denial and rejection, but through harmony.

The simple necessities of modern life would, however, force the college to face the problem of studies in its entire scope even if the philosophy of the sciences did not compel it. With the perspective of years, it will become clearer and clearer that the distinguishing characteristic of the nineteenth century is the development of applied science. The earlier years inherited the application to mechanics of the various uses of steam in the revolutionizing of industry. Succeeding years and decades

widened the application to practically all forms
of chemical and physical energy. The latter
decades saw the devolopment of the biological
sciences to the point of application. We do
not realize as yet the extent of the revolution
which the profession of medicine is undergoing because of the ability to make application
of chemistry, physiology, and bacteriology.
But it is not merely medicine, and public hygiene that are affected. Simple and fundamental industrial processes — agriculture, dai-
rying, etc.— are being invaded more and more
by applied science. The bacteriologist comes
home to us, not only in the treatment of dis-
ease, but in the making of our butter, and
cheese, and beer. The hour could be easily
spent in simply mentioning the multiple and
important points of contact between science
and the affairs of daily life. The beginning of
a new century surely sees us upon the verge of
an analogous translation of political and moral
science into terms of application.

Now it is absurd to the point of fatuity to
say, under such circumstances, we will restrict
our curriculum to a certain group of studies;
we will not introduce others · because they
have not been part of the classic curriculum
of the past, and consequently are not yet well
organized for educational purposes. The prob-

lem which the college has to face is not one
which has grown up within the college walls,
nor which is confined there. The ferment
which is happily going on in the college is
because the leaven of all modern life is at
work. There seems a certain lack of perspective, a certain lack of sanity and balance in
those arguments regarding the college curriculum that assume that subjects are already
in a settled condition; that there are ready-
made standards by which to measure their various claims; and that it only remains to pick
out just so much of this and so much of that
and put an end to all the confusion and conflict which is troubling us. Until the various
branches of human learning have attained
something like philosophic organization, until
the various modes of their application to life
have been so definitely and completely worked
out as to bring even the common affairs of
life under direction, confusion and conflict are
bound to continue. When we have an adequate industrial and political organization it
will be quite time to assume that there is
some offhand and short-cut solution to the
problem of educational organization. In the
meantime it is somewhat ridiculous to argue as
if there were somewhere a definite set of specific educational recipes which the managers of

the collegiate institutions might fall back upon,
and then serve out just such and such an intellectual diet to those eager for the intellectual
feast.

I have been speaking, thus far, of the problem as it presents itself on the side of the curriculum—on the side of the multiplication and
conflict of studies.   When we turn to the
matter of aims and methods, the moral end
and the fundamental intellectual attitude
involved, we do not find the state of things
much changed.   We talk, to be sure, about
character, and information, and discipline, and
culture as setting our aims and controlling our
methods.   We ignore the fact that every generation must redefine these terms for itself, if
they are to retain vitality.   We speak as if each
of these terms had a perfectly definite and
well-recognized meaning attaching to it ; we
appear to believe that some sort of mathemat-
ical ratio is possible—that by taking such a
per cent. of culture, such a per cent. of training,
such a per cent. of useful information, we may
get a well-rounded education.   Or, to take the
problem in its more burning form, we imagine
that we have just such and such a ratio between
the authoritative determination of material for
the student and his own personal choice—
assuming that there is a certain ratio between

external discipline and the play of individuality in the determination of character. All our universities are face to face, moreover, with the problem of the adjustment of what is ordinarily regarded as the strictly disciplinary and culture element in the curriculum to the professional element — the preparation for law, medicine, theology, or whatever. The common expedient, the device which works well on the practical side, is to allow the last year of the college course to count on both sides — for the degree which stands for general culture and discipline and also for the degree that stands for specific professional training. Turn from the matter of practical expediency and success to that of the philosophy of education, and what does this compromise mean? In terms of fundamental values, what is the relation between general culture and professional ability?

When we go below the surface, most of us, I think, would admit that we are in very great doubt as to what these terms really mean in themselves, to say nothing of their definite relationship to each other. What do we mean by character as a supreme end, or even incidental end, of college education? The topic lends itself gracefully to purposes of orations in which no cross-examination is permitted;

but suppose one of us had to answer, honestly and definitely, what he took to be the exact connection between each of the studies of the college course, and each daily lesson in each study, and the attainment of a right character—what would the answer be? Indeed, just exactly what is the character at which we are aiming, or ought to aim, under modern conditions? Character involves not only right intentions, but a certain degree of efficiency. Now efficiency, as biologists have made us well aware, is a problem of adaptation, of adjustment to the control of conditions. Are the conditions of modern life so clear and so settled that we know exactly what organs, what moral habits and methods, are necessary in order to get the maximum of efficiency? Do we know how to adjust our teaching to securing this maximum?

Great as are the difficulties in reaching an adequate definition of what we mean by character and its relation to education, the problem is slight compared with what meets us when we ask about the significance of the terms discipline and culture.

What is discipline? I find the same persons who, in one connection, emphasize the necessity of conducting education so as to give training, are often also the persons who, in another connection, object to a certain kind of work on the very ground that it gives too much and too specific training. He who upholds the banner of discipline in classics or mathematics, when it comes to the training of a man for the profession of a teacher or investigator, will often be found to condemn a school of commerce, or technology, or even of medicine, in the university on the ground that it is too professional in character—that it smacks of the utilitarian and commercial. The kind of discipline which enables a man to pursue one vocation is lauded; the kind of training that fits him for another is condemned. Why this invidious distinction? The only clew to an answer that I have ever been able to get is the assumption of some mysterious difference between a general training and a special training—as if the training that the man got in the study of Latin and Greek were somehow distinctively the training appropriate to man as man, while the training which he gets in the application of, say, mathematics and physics to engineering, or of history, geography, and political economy to commerce, only touches some narrow segment or fraction of the man. Whence the justification of any such assumption? Is not the whole man required in the calling of an engineer or a captain of industry?

If the whole man does not at present find opportunity and outlet for himself in these callings, is it not one of the main duties of the university to bring about precisely this result? The assumption that a training is good in general just in the degree in which it is good for nothing in particular is one for which it would be difficult to find any adequate philosophic ground. Training, discipline, must finally be measured in terms of application, of availability. To be trained is to be trained to something and for something.

This brings me to the question of culture. Doubtless, the current implication is that general culture and professional utility are quite independent of each other. The notion of absolute antagonism is, doubtless, wearing away. Like the similar conception of a fixed and obvious gulf between the elect and the unregenerated, it cannot stand the pressure of the free communication and interaction of modern life. It is no longer possible to hug complacently the ideal that the academic teacher is perforce devoted to high spiritual ideals, while the doctor, lawyer, and man of business are engaged in the mercenary pursuit of vulgar utilities. But we have hardly reconstructed our theory of the whole matter. Our conception of culture is still tainted with inheritance from the period of the aristocractic seclusion of a leisure class—leisure meaning relief from participation in the work of a workaday world. Culture, to use the happy phrase of one of my colleagues, has been prized largely as a means of "invidious distinction." If I were to venture into what might appear to you the metaphysical field, I think I could also show that the current idea of culture belongs to the pre-biological period—it is a survival of the time when mind was conceived as an independent entity living in an elegant isolation from its environment.

We come back here to the root of the whole matter. To very many the idea of culture covers adequately and completely that for which the college stands. Even to suggest that the college should do what the people want is to lay unholy hands on the sanctity of the college ideal. The people, the mob, the majority, want anything but culture—indeed they are capable of anything but culture. The college stands for the remnant. It is the fortress of the few who are capable of upholding high ideals against the utilitarian clamor of the many. To ask that the colleges do what society wants done is to surrender or compromise the idea of culture by requiring the introduction of the professional factor—a preparation for specific callings in life.

All this, I say frankly and emphatically, I regard as a survival from a dualistic past — from a society which was dualistic politically, drawing fixed lines between classes, and dualistic intellectually, with its rigid separation between the things of matter and of mind — between the affairs of the world and of the spirit. Social democracy means an abandonment of this dualism. It means a common heritage, a common work, and a common destiny. It is flat hostility to the ethics of modern life to suppose that there are two different aims of life located on different planes; that the few who are educated are to live on a plane of exclusive and isolated culture, while the many toil below on the level of practical endeavor directed at material commodity. The problem of our modern life is precisely to do away with all the barriers that keep up this division. If the university cannot accommodate itself to this movement, so much the worse for it. Nay, more; it is doomed to helpless failure unless it does more than accommodate itself; unless it becomes one of the chief agencies for bridging the gap, and bringing about an effective interaction of all callings in society.

This may seem pretty abstract, rather remote, in its actual bearing upon college affairs,

but there is a definite body of fact by which
to give this general statement concreteness.

I have already referred to the fact that we
are living in a period of applied science. What
this means for present purposes is that the
professions, the practical occupations of men,
are becoming less and less empirical routines,
or technical facilities acquired through unin-
telligent apprenticeship. They are more and
more infused with reason; more and more il-
luminated by the spirit of inquiry and reason.
They are dependent upon science, in a word.
To decline to recognize this intimate connection of professions in modern life with the
discipline and culture that come from the pursuit of truth for its own sake, is to be at least
one century behind the times. I do not say
that the engineer, the doctor, or lawyer, or
even the clergyman, or the average man of
commerce, has as yet awakened to the full
necessity of this interdependence of theory
and practice, to the full significance of the extent to which his activities are already dependent upon knowledge of the truth and the right
attitude toward truth. I do not say that the
professional classes are as yet fully aware of
the dignity and elevation that thus come to
their practical callings in life. But this very
absence of clear and complete consciousness

only makes the duty of the university the clearer. It is so to order its affairs that the availability of truth for life, and the dependence of the professional occupations upon science — upon insight into an ordered body of fact, and mastery of methods — shall become patent to all men.

Society needs the junction of that expert knowledge and skilled discipline which the college alone can supply, and the services of the professions, the businesses of life. All the forces and tendencies of college instruction and administration are tending irresistibly, even if blindly, in this direction. To say that the reality of the present university is professional training would perhaps give little other than material for misunderstanding. It would seem to mean that what most would regard as the important and essential feature of the university was a mere preliminary or incident, and that the reality is located in the schools of medicine, law, engineering, etc. This is not what is meant. I do mean, however, that the business of the university is coming to be more and more the supplying of that specific knowledge and that specific training which shall fit the individual for his calling in life. Just how the tendency shall work itself out on the formal and external side is a matter of com-

paratively little moment. The fact is sure
that the intellectual and moral lines which
divide the university courses in science and
letters from those of professional schools are
gradually getting obscure and are bound finally
to fade away.

What is termed general training and general
culture is the function of the secondary school.
A recent writer has stated that the college is
threatened with attack from two sources: the
high school on one side, the professional
school on the other. This exactly states the
situation to my mind—excepting that I should
not regard these instrumentalities as foes, but
rather as the twofold differentiation of function which the old-time amorphous college is
assuming.

Formally, the first two years of college
work probably belong to the secondary period.
This is not the place or time to go into the
question of what is meant by general training
and its relation to secondary-school work. It
certainly means, however, that the pupil shall
be touched, shall be stimulated, on all sides ;
that he shall be given a survey, at least, of the
universe in its manifold phases. Through this
survey, through this elaboration, coming to
know both himself and the universe, he may
get his orientation — his placing of himself in

the larger world. With proper economy of instruction, and harmonious organization instead of blind confusion in the curriculum, this result should certainly be attained by the time the average student is eighteen or twenty.

Having found himself, a student would then be prepared to enter upon that special training which is needed to equip him for the particular calling in life which he finds adapted to his own powers. This, by whatever name called, is professional training. The extent to which our larger universities have already moved in this direction is concealed, first, by the fact that they still retain considerable secondary work in the earlier years of their course ; and secondly, by the fact that training for the calling of teaching, or of special research, is marked off in the public mind from training for the calling of doctor, lawyer, or. engineer. In reality, the kind of training which students receive to make them professors, or directors of laboratories is, of course, as professional as is that of the school of technology or medicine.

There is still, however, a great deal of reconstructive work to be done. There is still a good deal of so-called higher college or university work which is thoroughly anomalous in character. It is neither one

thing nor the other. It does not give that
kind of education which awakens the student
to a sense of his own powers and their relation
to the world of action ; nor does it afford
specific training for any particular walk in life.
It is neither genuinely secondary nor yet mani-
festly collegiate in character. It is aimed in
the air with the pious hope that something
will come of it somewhere and somehow.
Those who insist on the maintenance of the
traditional college free from supposed en-
croachments of the high school on one side
and the professional school on the other, are
definitely contending, to my mind, for the per-
petuation of this amorphous and artifical thing.
Historically, the college, like the mediæval
university, was a great vocational institution.
Its original business was to prepare primarily
for the ministry, and incidentally for other
learned professions. That function gradually
departed from it, and it took on more and
more the form of an institution for general
culture. Now the high school is appropriat-
ing this function, and in its legitimate ex-
tension is bound to absorb more and more of
it. To give just more general culture at large,
after the specific period for it has ceased ; to
prepare in a loose and vague way for future
life — this is the anomaly to be corrected by

restoring to the college its position as a vocational institution.

The movement is steady and, I believe, inevitable in one direction. There is to be a
demarcation of the college into secondary
work on one side, and into training for vocations on the other. The secondary period will
be that of individual training and culture,
awakening the mind to true self-conscious-
ness—to a knowledge of self in its needs and
capacities in relation to life about it, thus
restoring to it freshness and vitality. The
collegiate institution will then be an affair for
specific training; for securing control of those
specialized systems of knowledge and methods
of research which fit the individual for the pursuit of his own calling in life.

All of us have callings, occupations — only
the luxuriously idle and the submerged idle,
only the leisure class of fashion and of pauper-
ism violate this law. When higher education
ceases to ignore the universality and significance, ethical as well as material, of this fact
of occupations, when it recognizes it frankly
and fully, and adapts its curriculum and
methods to it, the college will be coherent in
itself and in relation to the social whole. It
is movement in the direction of the union of
truth and use that defines the problems and
aims of the existing collegiate situation.